Contents

What is a mobile home?   6

Tents and shelters   8

Caravans and houseboats   10

Building a mobile home   12

Inside a mobile home   14

The weather   16

The environment   18

School and play   20

Going to work   22

Getting about   24

Where in the world?   26

Glossary   28

Further information   29

Index   30

Words in **bold** can be found in the glossary on page 28

What is a mobile home?

A mobile home is a home that can be moved from place to place. People need to move for many reasons. Some people move around to look for work. Other people move to new places to find food for their animals to eat.

▼ This home in Kalacha, Kenya is made from wooden poles covered with cloths. It is light and easy to move.

There are many kinds of mobile homes, including tents, houseboats and **yurts**. Some mobile homes have wheels. These homes are called **caravans**. They are **towed** along behind a car or other **vehicle**.

Mobile life

In the United States, a mobile home with its own motor is called a winnebago (win-ee-bay-go).

▲ This winnebago is travelling through the red rocks of the Valley of Fire State Park, in the United States.

Tents and shelters

Tents are easy and quick to put up and take down. People who live in tents are usually **nomads**. Nomads are people who move from one place to another, often to find grass for their animals to eat. Every time they move, they take their tents and all their **belongings** with them.

▼ This tent is in Tunisia in Africa. It belongs to nomads called the Bedouin people. The tent is made from camel hair.

A war or a disaster, such as an **earthquake**, can force people to leave their homes suddenly. People who are forced to leave their homes and live somewhere else are called **refugees**. They often live in **shelters** that can be moved easily.

▲ *These refugee families from Somalia have built their own shelters in a refugee camp in Ethiopia.*

Caravans and houseboats

Gypsies are nomads who live in Europe. In the past, they lived in brightly painted, wooden caravans pulled by horses. Today, many gypsies live in modern caravans. They have cars or vans to pull them along.

▼ *Every year gypsies meet at this horse fair held in Appleby in England.*

Mobile homes on the water are called houseboats. Some houseboats have their own motors to move around. Others have to be towed by other boats.

Mobile life
Traditional gypsy caravans are called vardos.

▲ A houseboat in Burleigh Falls, Canada. This houseboat has its own motor.

Building a mobile home

The Tuareg people live in the huge **desert** called the Sahara in northern Africa. They make their homes out of wooden poles for the **frame**. They stretch a cover made from goat skins across the poles.

▼ *The Tuareg use **woven** mats to make the sides of their shelters.*

In the Arctic, the Inuit people make shelters out of snow. These snowhouses are called **igloos**. Some Inuit people build igloos for shelter when they go on hunting trips in the winter. The thick snow blocks keep heat in better than a tent during the Arctic winter.

▲ *These Inuit people in Quebec, Canada, are cutting blocks out of the deep snow to build an igloo.*

Inside a mobile home

Across Central Asia, people live in mobile homes called yurts. A yurt is built in the shape of a circle. The wall is a criss-cross frame made out of wood from willow trees and covered in thick **felt** mats. The floor is covered in rugs for warmth.

▼ *This yurt is in Uzbekistan. People sit on the floor of the yurt to eat their meals.*

In some mobile homes, everything has to be squeezed into a small space. In camper vans, people can sit on long seats during the daytime. At night, the seats pull across to make a bed.

▲ *This camper van has lots of cupboards above the windows to store things.*

The weather

Tents are useful mobile homes in hot, dry places, such as deserts. People can put up a tent in the **shade** of a tree to keep it cool. They can open the side of the tent to let cool air in. Or they can shut the tent to keep strong winds out.

▼ *The tent on this van is used for camping in Australia. Air flows around the tent to keep it cool.*

Mobile homes are sometimes used in wet, rainy places. The Mbuti people live in the **rainforest** in the middle of Africa. They make their homes out of wooden frames covered with large leaves.

▲ The large leaves covering these homes in Ituri forest, Zaire, help to keep the rain out.

The environment

When summer ends some nomads move to warmer places. In Mongolia, many nomads spend the summer in the mountains. Their cows, sheep and goats eat the grass in the high **pastures**. Then they pack up their homes and move to lower pastures for the cold winter months.

▼ *In Mongolia, nomads move their yurts with the **seasons**. These yurts stand in the snow near Lake Tsagaan Nuur.*

Hurricanes and strong winds can do lots of damage to mobile homes. Mobile homes are usually made from light materials, such as wood, metal or plastic, so that people can move them easily. They are not as strong as houses made from stone or brick.

▲ Trailer homes in this park in North America were completely destroyed by a hurricane.

School and play

Children who live in mobile homes may move around a lot. When they move, they cannot go to the same school all the time. Parents may teach their children at home. Refugee camps sometimes have schools so children can learn while they are far from home.

▼ These children go to school in a refugee camp in Nepal, at least 200 kilometres away from where they used to live.

Mobile homes are often quite small, so children spend a lot of time playing outside. Children from families that move around often play together and become good friends.

▲ *Children play outside a gypsy campsite in Lourdes, France.*

Going to work

Many people who move from place to place are farmers. When they move they look for new land to **graze** their animals, or a place to grow their crops. When the grass or the soil gets worn out in one place, the farmer looks for new land to start again.

▼ *This farmer is burning a patch of rainforest in Brazil to clear a space to grow crops.*

A circus is a group of people who travel around and put on shows in lots of towns and villages. They include clowns, acrobats and jugglers and they live in caravans. The circus happens in a big tent, called a big top.

▲ *The big top is surrounded by caravans, where people who work for the circus live.*

Getting about

In deserts, people use camels or donkeys to carry their homes from place to place. They fold up their homes and put them on the camels' backs. Camels are very strong and they can carry heavy loads in hot deserts.

▼ *These camels are carrying the frames and mats of Gabbra houses in Maikona, Kenya.*

In the Arctic, the Inuit used to travel across the ice and snow on **sledges** pulled by dogs. Today, most Inuit use sledges with motors, called **skidoos**.

Mobile life

Camels have very wide feet so they can walk on the soft desert sand without sinking.

▲ *Inuit people drive their skidoos across the ice in Igloolik, Canada. The ice is melting because it is summer.*

Where in the world?

Some of the places talked about in this book have been labelled here.

Look at these two pictures carefully.

- How are the homes different from each other?

- What is each home made of?

- Look at their walls and roofs.

- How are these homes different from where you live?

- How are they the same?

Igloolik

NORTH AMERICA

Burleigh Falls

Valley of Fire State Park

ATLANTIC OCEAN

PACIFIC OCEAN

SOUTH AMERICA

Quebec, Canada

N
W   E
S

ASIA

*Lake
Tsagaan
Nuur*

•Appleby

EUROPE

urdes
•

*SAHARA
DESERT*

AFRICA

Ituri •
forest   • Maikona

PACIFIC

OCEAN

AUSTRALASIA

ANTARCTICA

Kalacha, Kenya

Glossary

belongings	the things that people own
caravan	a mobile home on wheels
desert	a dry area with very little or no rainfall
earthquake	when the earth moves and shakes
felt	a thick, warm fabric made from wool or animal hair
frame	a structure that gives something shape and strength
graze	to eat grass
gypsies	people who live as nomads in Europe
hurricane	a strong storm with high winds and lots of rain
igloo	a snowhouse
nomads	people who move from place to place rather than living in one place all the time
pasture	land covered with grass where animals go to graze
rainforest	an area of thick forest with high rainfall in a tropical region
refugees	people who are forced to leave their homes and live somewhere else
seasons	four different times of year, with different kinds of weather. The seasons are winter, spring, summer and autumn.
shade	an area where there is no sun
shelter	any structure that provides some cover from the weather
skidoo	a sledge with a motor
sledge	a vehicle with runners for moving across snow
tow	to pull something behind you
vehicle	any kind of transport with wheels, such as a car or a truck
woven	when something has been threaded in and out
yurt	a kind of mobile home used in Central Asia

Further information

Books to read

Starters: Homes Rosie McCormick, Wayland (2003)
Around the World: Homes Margaret Hall, Heinemann (2003)
One Day We Had to Run Sybella Wilkes, Evans (2000)

Websites

http://www.ucc.uconn.edu/~epsadm03/mbuti.html
For information about the Mbuti of Zaire

http://kids.mongabay.com/elementary/001.html
For information about rainforests

http://collections.ic.gc.ca/arctic/inuit/people.htm
For information about the Inuit

http://www.mongolyurt.com/
For information about yurts

Index

All the numbers in **bold** refer to photographs.

A
animals 6, 8, **8**, 18, 22, 24, **24**, 25
B
Bedouin 8, **8**
C
camper vans 15, **15**
caravans 7, **7**, 10, **10**, 11, 23, **23**
children 20-21, **20-21**
circus 23, **23**
cloths 6, **6**, 27
D
deserts 12, 24, 25
F
farmers 22, **22**

G
gypsies 10, **10**, 11
H
houseboats 7, 11, **11**
hurricanes 19, **19**
I
igloos 13, **13**, **26**
Inuit 13, **13**, 25, **25**, **26**
M
mats 12, **12**, 14, **14**
Mbuti 17, **17**
N
nomads 8, **8**, 10, **10**, 18
R
rainforests 17, **17**
refugee camps 9, **9**, 20, **20**
refugees 9, **9**, 20, **20**
rugs 14, **14**

S
schools 20, **20**
seasons 18, 25
skidoos 25, **25**
snow 13, **13**, 18, **18**, **26**
T
tents 7, 8, **8**, 16, **16**
Tuareg 12
W
winnebagos 7, **7**
wooden poles 6, **6**, 12, **12**, 14, **14**, 17, **17**, **27**
Y
yurts 7, 14, **14**, 15, 18, **18**